Ideas, Inventions, and Innovators

PEOPLE WHO CHANGED THE WORLD

SCIENCE AND ARTS

BY GRACE JONES

CRABTREE
PUBLISHING COMPANY
WWW.CRABTREEBOOKS.COM

CRABTREE
PUBLISHING COMPANY
WWW.CRABTREEBOOKS.COM

Published in Canada
Crabtree Publishing
616 Welland Avenue
St. Catharines, ON
L2M 5V6

Published in the United States
Crabtree Publishing
PMB 59051
350 Fifth Ave, 59th Floor
New York, NY 10118

Published in 2019 by Crabtree Publishing Company

Author: Grace Jones

Editorial director: Kathy Middleton

Editors: Kirsty Holmes, Petrice Custance

Proofreader: Melissa Boyce

Designer: Matt Rumbelow

Prepress technicians: Tammy McGarr, Ken Wright

Print coordinator: Katherine Berti

Images

Shutterstock: JStone, cover (top left), title page (left), pp 5 (bottom
right), 25 (bottom right), 28 (top right); drserg pp 5 (4th row, middle),
26 (top right); Oleg Golovnev p 6 (bottom right); Igor Bulgarin p 8
(bottom right); Claudio Divizia p 9 (top right); Kamira p 9 (middle right);
p 13; Forty3Zero p 25 (top); Philip Pilosian p 25 (bottom left); Life In
Pixels p 28 (bottom); s_bukley p 29 (top); landmarkmedia p 29 (bottom
left)

Wikimedia: pp 5 (2nd row left), 12 (right); LOC pp 5 (3rd row left),
18 (right); pp 5 (3rd row, middle), 21 (top right); United States public
domain pp 5 (3rd row, right), 22 (top right); pp 5 (4th row, left), 24
(bottom right); p 12 (left); p 18 (bottom right); 20 (left); public domain
p 21 (bottom); p 22 (left); Massimo Catarinella p 22 (bottom); Heather
Cowper p 23 (top); p 23 (bottom); Gerrit de Bruin p 24 (top); Roland
Godefroy p 25 (middle)

All other images from Shutterstock

All facts, statistics, web addresses and URLs in this book were verified
as valid and accurate at time of writing. No responsibility for any
changes to external websites or references can be accepted by either
the author or publisher.

Printed in the U.S.A./122018/CG20181005

Library and Archives Canada Cataloguing in Publication

Jones, Grace, 1990-, author
    People who changed the world : science and arts / Grace Jones.

(Ideas, inventions, and innovators)
Includes index.
Issued in print and electronic formats.
ISBN 978-0-7787-5828-0 (hardcover).--
ISBN 978-0-7787-5971-3 (softcover).--
ISBN 978-1-4271-2239-1 (HTML)

    1. Scientists--Miscellanea--Juvenile literature. 2. Science--History--
Miscellanea--Juvenile literature. 3. Artists--Miscellanea--Juvenile
literature. 4. Art--History--Miscellanea--Juvenile literature. I. Title.

Q163.J66 2018   j509.2'2   C2018-905464-6
                                           C2018-905465-4

Library of Congress Cataloging-in-Publication Data

Names: Jones, Grace, 1990- author.
Title: People who changed the world : science and arts / Grace Jones.
Description: New York, New York : Crabtree Publishing Company, 2019.
 | Series: Ideas, inventions, and innovators | Includes index.
Identifiers: LCCN 2018043643 (print) | LCCN 2018047413 (ebook) |
 ISBN 9781427122391 (Electronic) |
 ISBN 9780778758280 (hardcover) |
 ISBN 9780778759713 (pbk.)
Subjects: LCSH: Scientists--Biography--Juvenile literature. |
 Authors--Biography--Juvenile literature. | Musicians--Biography--
 Juvenile literature.
Classification: LCC Q141 (ebook) | LCC Q141 .J685 2019 (print) |
 DDC 509.2/2--dc23
LC record available at https://lccn.loc.gov/2018043643

CONTENTS

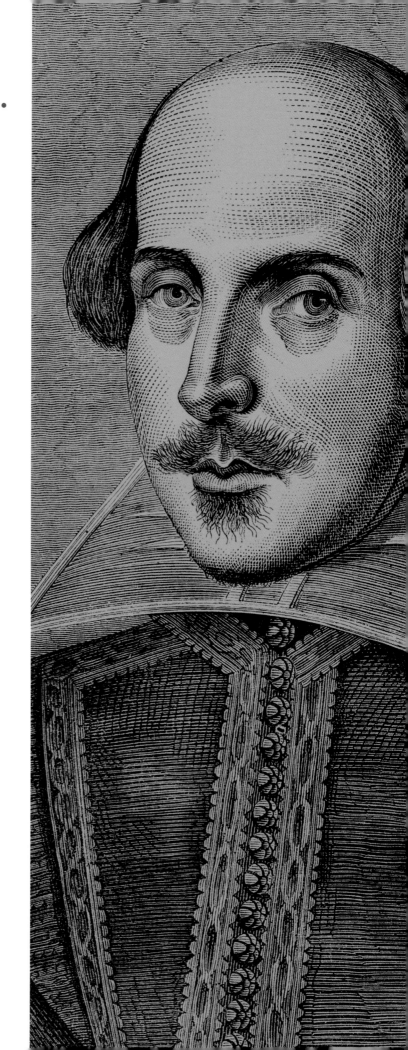

PEOPLE WHO CHANGED THE WORLD

• •

Over hundreds of years, humans have achieved many extraordinary **feats**, from making groundbreaking discoveries to dreaming up fantastic stories and providing inspiration and hope to people around the world. This book will profile just a few of the incredible people throughout history who, working in the sciences and arts, have changed people's lives forever.

Why is Leonardo da Vinci called a Renaissance Man?

How did Shakespeare's plays change the world?

What shocked Benjamin Franklin?

Why was Ada Lovelace one hundred years before her time?

How did Florence Nightingale help the sick and injured?

How did Marie Curie help us look inside the human body?

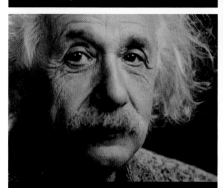

How did Albert Einstein change the way we view the world?

What contribution did Sidney Poitier make to movies?

Why is Anne Frank so inspirational to so many people?

How did Nina Simone's music influence the world?

How did Sir Tim Berners-Lee get us all online?

How did J.K. Rowling cast a spell over the way we read?

Let's go on a journey to find the answers to these questions and more...

5

LEONARDO DA VINCI

· ·

Leonardo da Vinci was born in 1452 in Vinci, Italy. From an early age, Leonardo showed he had artistic talent. At 14 years old, he began to work in Florence for the famous artist Andrea del Verrocchio. During this time, he developed a wide range of artistic skills, including painting, sculpting, drawing, and even **carpentry**.

Replica of an artist's workshop from the time of da Vinci.

Although not many of da Vinci's original drawings, paintings, and sculptures remain in existence, he is still considered to be one of the greatest artists who ever lived. One of the most famous paintings in the world, the *Mona Lisa*, was painted by da Vinci. The painting is located in the Louvre Museum in Paris, and receives more than six million visitors every year. Experts estimate the painting is worth nearly $800 million.

Da Vinci painted in the **Renaissance** style. The Renaissance period was a time of discovery and observation in the sciences and arts, with a focus on revealing truth.

In 1482, da Vinci was offered a job with the Duke of Milan. Da Vinci worked for him as a painter, sculptor, and even as an inventor. Da Vinci invented and sketched war machines for the Duke. He also designed very early versions of the bicycle, helicopter, and airplane—in the 1400s! Da Vinci was not just a great artist. He is also recognized as a great inventor and scientist.

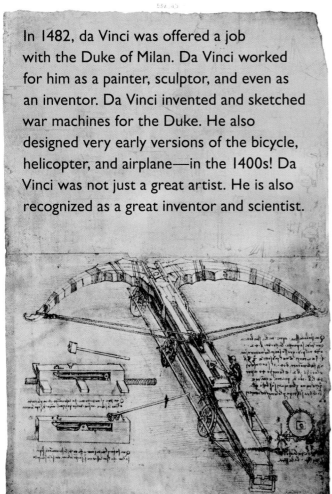

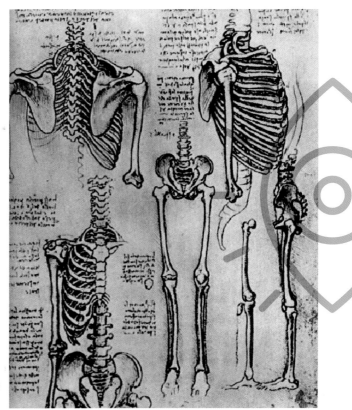

Da Vinci was very interested in the science of the body. He made many sketches of body parts.

Leonardo da Vinci was one of the greatest artists in history. He inspired many artists while he lived, and he continues to inspire today. Da Vinci's achievements in many different fields have earned him the modern-day nickname "Renaissance Man."

WILLIAM SHAKESPEARE

• •

William Shakespeare was born in 1564 in Stratford-upon-Avon, England. His father was a business owner and his mother was the daughter of a landowner. At age 18, Shakespeare married Anne Hathaway, and the couple had three children. At some point after marrying, Shakespeare moved to London to write and act in plays. Nothing is known about him between the years 1585 and 1592.

Not much is known about Shakespeare's education, but it is likely his parents were able to pay for him to have a good education.

When in London, Shakespeare worked as an actor for a company called the Lord Chamberlain's Men. He also wrote plays for the company that were popular and interesting to many people at the time. His early plays were mainly comedies such as *Much Ado About Nothing*, or plays that focused on certain parts of history, such as *Henry V*.

Shakespeare also wrote many poems in his lifetime and published 150 **sonnets**. Many of them are still very famous today.

In 1598, the Lord Chamberlain's Men was in danger of losing its theater due to an argument over the **lease**. To prevent this, the actors took apart the building and moved it across the Thames River. The new theater, called the Globe Theatre, was circular, with three levels of audience seating. There was also a pit in front of the stage, where people could buy cheaper tickets and stand for performances. The plays at the Globe Theatre became very popular, and were usually sold out.

It is during this time that Shakespeare is considered to have written his greatest plays, including *Hamlet*, *King Lear*, and *Macbeth*.

All the World's a Stage

Shakespeare died in 1616, but his **legacy** continues. He is considered to be the greatest and most **influential** playwright in history. His influence was so great that many students still study his work in schools and universities all over the world. His plays continue to be made into films and performed in theaters worldwide.

Shakespeare is said to have written 38 plays in his lifetime.

BENJAMIN FRANKLIN

Benjamin Franklin was a scientist who is considered to be the first person to discover how to use electricity. Franklin's discovery has changed the lives of everyone on the planet. It's the reason why we now have electric lights instead of candles, and it allows us to watch television and use our cell phones.

Franklin developed an idea that electricity can flow between two points. He thought that lightning might be one example of this theory, so in 1752 he performed an experiment to prove it.

When one object is rubbed against another, electricity can be created. Believe it or not, this is not a magic trick—it is just **static electricity** at work.

In order to prove that lightning was electricity flowing between two points, Franklin flew a kite during a thunderstorm. He tied an iron key to the bottom of the kite string and an iron rod to the top of the kite.

Electricity from the clouds flowed into the iron rod, down the kite string, and into the key he was holding. Because metal is a **conductor** of electricity, Franklin received an electric shock, which proved his theory to be correct! Luckily, his kite wasn't hit by lightning, as that amount of electricity would have killed him. It is always very dangerous to experiment with electricity in any way.

Franklin went on to invent many more things during his lifetime, including a type of glasses called bifocals, and a glass harmonica. He also made many other discoveries about electricity, weather, cooling, and light.

Benjamin Franklin was one of the Founding Fathers of the United States. In 1776, he helped write the American Declaration of Independence.

ADA LOVELACE

Ada Lovelace, known as the mother of computer programming, was born in 1815 in London, England. That may seem strange, given that modern computers were developed in the 1940s, but it is true! Ada Lovelace was the first known person to believe that machines could do more than calculate numbers.

This version of Babbage's analytical engine was built in 1910.

Lovelace was the daughter of the famous English poet, Lord Byron. From her father she inherited a creative mind. Under her mother's influence, she developed a strong interest in math and science, which was uncommon for women at that time. Lovelace became friends with Charles Babbage, the English mathematician who today is known as the father of computing. Knowing Lovelace's interest in math and science, Babbage asked her to translate an article written in Italian about his plans to build an **analytical** engine.

The idea of Babbage's analytical engine fascinated Lovelace. Recognized today as a plan for the earliest version of a computer, the mechanical engine would be powered by steam and be able to perform mathematical functions through the use of punched cards. The punched cards were pieces of paper with holes punched in particular places. When fed into the analytical engine, the placement of the holes on the cards would instruct the machine on how to function.

While Babbage concentrated only on the mathematical possibilities of his engine, Lovelace recognized it would be able to do much more, such as compose music.

Punched cards

Diagram for the computation by the Engine of the Numbers of Bernoulli. See Note G. (page 722 et seq.)

Ada's algorithm

In the 1970s, the United States Department of Defense developed a computer programming language for its systems. They named it Ada.

Lovelace wrote her own lengthy notes to be included with the translation of the article about the analytical engine. In those notes, Lovelace included an **algorithm**, which is now considered the first computer program ever written. Published in 1843, Lovelace's notes were very well received. The analytical engine was never built, but the ideas behind it lived on.

One hundred years later, Lovelace's work inspired an English mathematician named Alan Turing, who is credited with developing the computer as we know it today.

FLORENCE NIGHTINGALE

Florence Nightingale was born in 1820 in Italy to British parents. From an early age, Nightingale helped to look after the sick and poor in her neighborhood. As she grew older, she believed she was meant to be a nurse. Nightingale began her training in 1850. After finishing, she worked in several hospitals and was quickly recognized for her impressive work in improving **hygiene** practices and saving lives.

Florence Nightingale was named after the city where she was born—Florence, Italy.

In 1854, the British Secretary of War requested that Nightingale organize a group of nurses to look after the sick and injured from the **Crimean War**. When Nightingale arrived, she was shocked by the filthy and unhygienic conditions she found there. Patients were lying in their own waste, rodents were running around, and the hospital lacked basic medical supplies, such as bandages.

More soldiers were dying from diseases than from their battle injuries.

Nightingale ordered that the hospital be cleaned from top to bottom. Then Nightingale, the other nurses, and even some of the healthier patients worked to keep the hospital clean. In the evenings, Nightingale would carry a lamp as she visited each patient. The soldiers nicknamed her the "Lady with the Lamp." Through her hard work, **compassion**, and dedication to improving the hygiene and care conditions at the hospital, she reduced the death rate by over two-thirds.

St. Thomas' Hospital

As well as the "Lady with the Lamp," Florence Nightingale's grateful patients also called her the "Angel of Crimea."

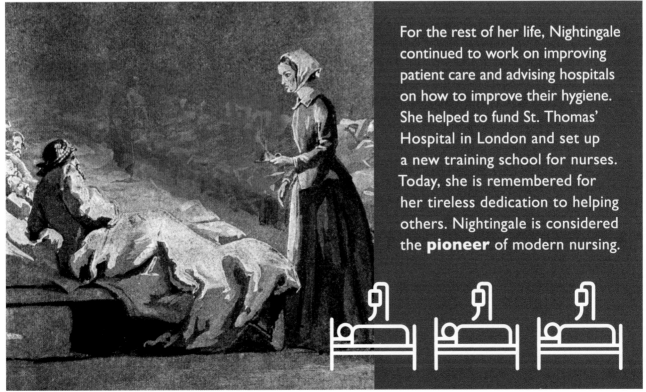

For the rest of her life, Nightingale continued to work on improving patient care and advising hospitals on how to improve their hygiene. She helped to fund St. Thomas' Hospital in London and set up a new training school for nurses. Today, she is remembered for her tireless dedication to helping others. Nightingale is considered the **pioneer** of modern nursing.

MARIE CURIE

In 1896, a French scientist named Henri Becquerel discovered that an **element** called uranium **emitted** energetic **particles**, or active rays. Marie Curie, a French-Polish scientist, was interested in Becquerel's discovery and wanted to find out more.

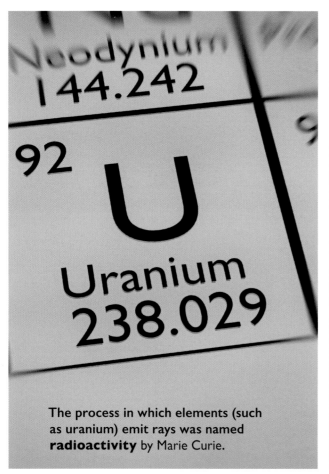

The process in which elements (such as uranium) emit rays was named **radioactivity** by Marie Curie.

Marie Curie, alongside her husband Pierre Curie, began to experiment with uranium. During one experiment, she noted that the material left after she removed the uranium seemed to be more active than the uranium itself. She decided there must be other more active elements contained within the material. Her theory was right, and in 1898, Marie and Pierre discovered two new radioactive elements, polonium and radium.

Today, we use uranium to generate electricity in nuclear power stations.

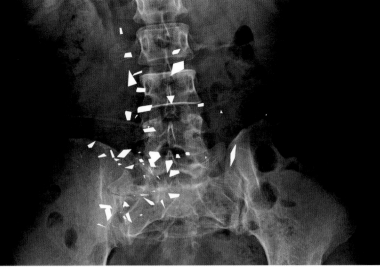

During the rest of her life, Curie worked on researching the uses and properties of radium. She also helped to save millions of lives in **World War I** by developing **portable** X-ray machines that could locate the positions of **shrapnel** in soldiers' bodies, which doctors could then remove. She died in 1934 of cancer, probably due to her exposure to **radiation** for many years.

Marie Curie was the first woman to win the **Nobel Prize**. She won the Nobel Prize in Physics, along with her husband, in 1903. She is also the only woman to win it twice. She won the Nobel Prize in Chemistry in 1911.

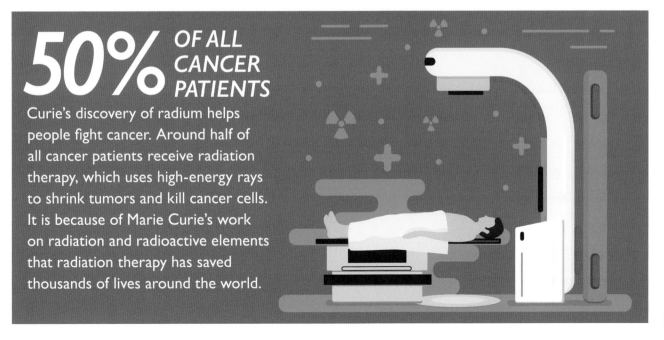

50% OF ALL CANCER PATIENTS

Curie's discovery of radium helps people fight cancer. Around half of all cancer patients receive radiation therapy, which uses high-energy rays to shrink tumors and kill cancer cells. It is because of Marie Curie's work on radiation and radioactive elements that radiation therapy has saved thousands of lives around the world.

ALBERT EINSTEIN

• •

Albert Einstein was born in 1879 in Ulm, Germany. From a young age, Einstein was interested in science and math. When he was older, he began to study for a degree in physics at university in Zurich, Switzerland. Once finished, he began to work in an office, but continued to study physics.

UNIVERSITÄT ZÜRICH ZENTRUM

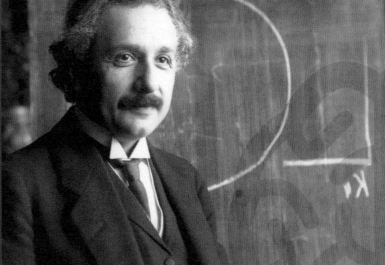

Einstein's experiments were very important. He had many theories about the way light and time actually work. For example, his theories of **relativity** showed how the speed of light is fixed, but space and time are not fixed—they can bend! He also showed that space and time are part of the same thing, which he called spacetime.

With such an amazing mind, Einstein quickly became a famous scientist. He worked on many important ideas, mostly about things such as light and **gravity**. Einstein was Jewish, so in 1933, when the **Nazi** party was in power in Germany, he left Europe to live and work in the United States. He went on to win a Nobel Prize for Physics. His most famous formula is E=mc², which is a complicated theory meaning that **mass** can be turned into energy. Even something very small, such as an **atom**, can make a huge amount of energy!

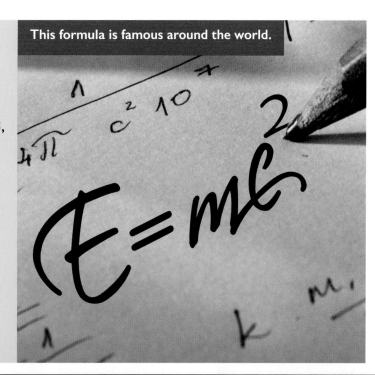
This formula is famous around the world.

Albert Einstein is considered to be one of the most important scientists in the history of the world. He made many discoveries in his lifetime, including his special theory of relativity. He proved the existence of the atom and changed the way in which scientists viewed the world. He also influenced many future discoveries and inventions. Televisions and computers are just some of the things that we might not have without Einstein's work.

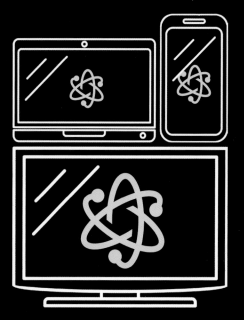

SIDNEY POITIER

. . . .

In 1964, Sidney Poitier was the first black man to win the Academy Award for Best Actor. He was one of the most popular stars in Hollywood in the 1960s, and Poitier was determined to use his status to erase damaging **stereotypes** of black people that had been seen onscreen since movies began.

Sidney Poitier was supposed to be born in his homeland, the Bahamas. However, during a trip to Miami, Florida in 1927, his mother went into premature labor, making Poitier an American citizen. He was raised in the Bahamas until he was 15, when he went to live with an older brother in Florida. This was when Poitier encountered racism for the first time in his life, which shocked him. He decided he wanted to try acting, and soon moved to New York City. Poitier used to listen to the radio for hours, practicing words over and over in an attempt to lose his Bahamian accent.

In 1950, Poitier was cast in his first movie. In 1963, he starred in *Lilies of the Field*, which earned him the Academy Award. Poitier appealed to both black and white audiences, and for much of the 1960s he was the top box office earner.

In 1967, Poitier starred in three groundbreaking films that challenged racism: *To Sir, with Love*, *In the Heat of the Night*, and *Guess Who's Coming to Dinner*. In these films, Poitier was not only the lead, but also dignified and elegant. This was significant, because black people had not often seen themselves portrayed on the screen that way before. This was happening at the same time as the **civil rights movement**.

Poitier marked an important turning point for black people in Hollywood. However, more than forty years later, the popularity of the **hashtag #OscarsSoWhite** proves there is still much progress to be made.

Poitier with fellow actors on August 28, 1963, at the **March on Washington**, in Washington, D.C.

In 2009, Sidney Poitier was awarded the Presidential Medal of Freedom by President Barack Obama, the highest civilian award of the United States.

ANNE FRANK

• •

She only lived 15 years, but Anne Frank's hope and wisdom have inspired milllons around the world. *The Diary of a Young Girl*, published in English in 1952, is the diary Anne Frank kept during her years living in hiding from the Nazis during **World War II**. The young Jewish girl's thoughts on life, love, and the effects of war have been published in 70 languages, with over 30 million copies sold.

Anne Frank was born in Germany in 1929. In 1933, after the Nazis took control of Germany, the Frank family moved to Amsterdam, Netherlands. The Nazis invaded the Netherlands in 1940, making Amsterdam unsafe for the Jewish family. On July 6, 1942, the Frank family went into hiding in a secret living area in the back of the building where Anne's father worked. Four other Jewish people joined them in the secret space.

Anne's secret hiding place in Amsterdam.

During the two years Anne lived in hiding, she kept a diary. In that diary she discussed her hopes and dreams, her feelings about her family and others in the hiding space, and her thoughts about the war and what was happening to Jewish people. Despite the scary conditions in which she was living, Anne's writing was incredibly uplifting and positive.

On August 4, 1944, an anonymous tip led the Nazis to the secret hiding space. All eight of the group were arrested and transported to Nazi **concentration camps**. Of the eight, only Anne's father survived. Anne died in March 1945 of **typhus**. When Anne's father returned to Amsterdam after the war, friends who had collected their personal items handed him Anne's diary.

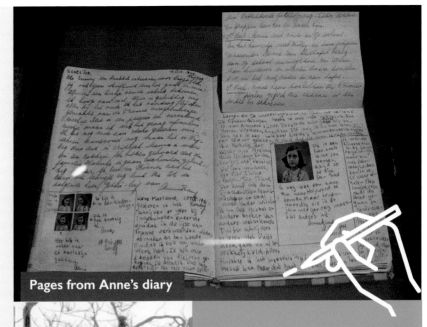

Pages from Anne's diary

"**Think of all the beauty still left around you and be happy.**"

Anne Frank, from *The Diary of a Young Girl*

While in hiding, Anne often looked out the window at a large chestnut tree, which she loved. Anne Frank House, the museum now located at Anne's secret hiding space, has created **saplings** from that tree. They have now been planted around the world, including in the United States and Canada.

NINA SIMONE

Eunice Kathleen Waymon, now known as Nina Simone, was born in North Carolina in 1933 to a poor family. She started to learn how to play the piano at the age of three. After deciding that she wanted to become a pianist, a music teacher helped to pay for her musical education. When she was older, Simone could not afford music school and had to drop out.

Early on, she took the stage name Nina Simone because some family members disapproved of her performing in public.

Nina Simone was nicknamed "the High Priestess of Soul."

In the 1950s, without money and unable to study music, Simone started playing piano and singing in jazz and blues clubs in Atlantic City. Simone gained popularity over the years and signed a record deal. She released her first album in 1958. Nina Simone went on to produce many albums that covered many different **genres** of music, such as jazz, blues, folk, and classical.

In the 1960s, Simone became the musical voice of the civil rights movement. Many of her songs were about racial discrimination and the problems black Americans faced within society.
As well as writing music, Simone was also an active civil rights protester.

Nina Simone struggled with mental illness, especially in her later life, and was eventually diagnosed with **bipolar disorder** in the 1980s.

Nina Simone inspired a whole generation of musicians that followed, including The Beatles, Elton John, Madonna, and Beyoncé. Her work continues to inspire people and musicians alike. She also leaves a strong legacy in the world of political activism and the fight for equal rights.

25

SIR TIM BERNERS-LEE

• •

Some inventions completely change people's lives. In 1989, Tim Berners-Lee invented the World Wide Web. Since then, the way many people around the world go about their daily lives has completely changed—from how we communicate with loved ones or purchase a book to the ability to work from home.

Tim Berners-Lee was working for a company when his earliest ideas of the Internet were formed. He found it frustrating that he had to get different information on different computers, each using a different program that he had to learn. He had an idea to create one system on which all people could access all information at all times. Berners-Lee turned his idea into a reality and created the World Wide Web.

Berners-Lee created an information space where people could access and share documents, images, videos, and audio files. This **virtual** space, the Internet, has allowed people to communicate much more easily with one another and has provided access to huge amounts of information. Today, we use the Internet to do practically everything—to order food, buy clothes, and even help us do our homework.

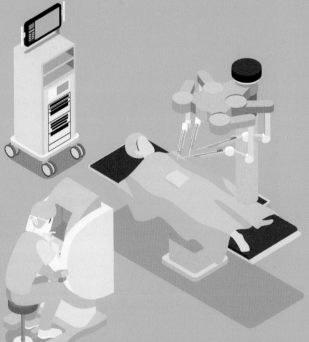

The Internet has given people access to an enormous amount of human knowledge. This has enabled people to learn and develop many new technologies, such as instant messaging, video calling, and even the ability for a surgeon to perform an operation on a person far away, using a robot! The Internet is an important invention because it has connected us all.

Berners-Lee was the first person to invent the Internet, but much of the technology he used for it had already been invented by others. He put it all together and changed the world!

KNOWLEDGE

J.K. ROWLING

One day in 1990, Joanne Rowling was traveling on a train from Manchester to London, England. On that journey, she thought of an idea for a book. It was about a young wizard who lived in a magical world. After the journey, she put pen to paper and started to write the book.

After years of writing, Rowling finished her first book. At that time, she was living in Scotland and was struggling to support herself and her daughter. She took her manuscript to many publishers who rejected it, until one editor, Barry Cunningham, finally accepted it. The book was published in the United States in 1998 as *Harry Potter and the Sorcerer's Stone*.

After the first *Harry Potter* book was published, Rowling won many book awards. She went on to write six more books in the series, achieving worldwide fame and fortune.

80 500 766 11

Translated into 80 languages

More than 500 million books sold

Of all seven books in the series, *Harry Potter and the Order of the Phoenix* is the longest, with 766 pages in the UK version.

Harry Potter and the Deathly Hallows sold 11 million copies in the first 24 hours of its release.

The *Harry Potter* series has now been made into eight hugely successful films starring the actors Emma Watson as Hermione Granger, Daniel Radcliffe as Harry Potter, and Rupert Grint as Ron Weasley. The *Harry Potter* books, films, and merchandise are estimated to be worth $25 billion. It is estimated that Rowling herself has earned nearly $1 billion.

J.K. Rowling is involved with many charities. In 2011 alone, she donated more than $150 million. She is also considered by many to be the most influential writer in the world.

The *Harry Potter* books sparked an interest in reading for children at a time when the number of children reading was decreasing. Rowling also captivated children and adults alike with the magic of her writing and the fantastical world that she created.

29

GLOSSARY

#OscarsSoWhite A hashtag used to protect the lack of minorities in films

algorithm A set of steps to follow in order to solve a mathematical problem or to complete a computer process

analytical Having the skill to think or reason

atom The smallest possible part of anything

bipolar disorder A mental health illness causing severe mood changes

carpentry The process of building or repairing things made of wood

civil rights movement Organized activities in the 1950s and 1960s that demanded racial equality for black Americans

compassion Care and concern for the suffering of others

concentration camp A camp where people are held prisoner for political reasons

conductor A material that allows heat or electricity to pass through it

Crimean War A conflict lasting from 1853 to 1856 between the Russian Empire and Britain, France, and Turkey

element A basic substance that is one of the building blocks for all matter on Earth

emitted Released something

feats Impressive accomplishments

genres Specific types of film, music, or writing

gravity The force that pulls two objects toward each other

hashtag A word or phrase that begins with the symbol #, classifying it for social media

hygiene Maintaining health through cleanliness

influential Having the power to cause change

lease A legal agreement that allows someone to rent something for a period of time

legacy Something that is passed on

Nazi The German political party of Adolph Hitler during World War II, responsible for the murder of millions, including 6 million Jewish people

March on Washington The political demonstration held on August 28, 1963 in Washington, D.C. demanding civil rights for black Americans

mass A measure of how much matter is in an object

Nobel Prize An annual prize for outstanding work in physics, chemistry, medicine, literature, economics, and peace

particles Tiny bits of matter that cannot be split into smaller parts

pioneer The first person to begin or develop something

LEARNING MORE

portable Capable of being carried or moved

radiation Energy that moves from one place to another

radioactivity Breaking apart atoms to give off energy

relativity A theory developed by Albert Einstein relating to the way anything except light moves through space and time

Renaissance A time period, generally between 1400 and 1600, when great advancements were made in science and art

replica A copy of an original

saplings Young plants grown from seeds

shrapnel Parts from an exploded bomb

sonnets Poems that have 14 lines and are usually about love

static electricity Electricity created by two objects rubbing against each other

stereotype A too simplistic or unfair belief about someone or something

typhus A disease transmitted by body lice

virtual Existing only online

World War I A global conflict that lasted from 1914 to 1918

World War II A global conflict that lasted from 1939 to 1945

BOOKS

Dakers, Diane. *Albert Einstein: Forging the Path of Modern Physics.* Crabtree Publishing, 2014.

Dakers, Diane. *Elie Wiesel: Holocaust Survivor and Messenger for Humanity.* Crabtree Publishing, 2012.

Noyce, Pendred. *Magnificent Minds: 16 Pioneering Women in Science and Medicine.* Tumblehome Learning, 2016.

WEBSITES

Visit this site to learn more about the civil rights movement:
www.ducksters.com/history/ civil_rights/african-american_civil_ rights_movement.php

Learn more about Leonardo da Vinci here:
www.coolkidfacts.com/leonardo-da-vinci-facts/

Learn more about physics and the work of Marie Curie and Albert Einstein here:
www.ducksters.com/science/physics/

INDEX